ONE LITTLE
**YES**
CAN CHANGE
YOUR LIFE

# ONE LITTLE
# YES
# CAN CHANGE
# YOUR LIFE

*Excerpts from*
### The GRAVE
### ROBBER

# MARK BATTERSON

**BakerBooks**
*a division of Baker Publishing Group*
Grand Rapids, Michigan

© 2014 by Mark Batterson

Published by Baker Books
a division of Baker Publishing Group
P.O. Box 6287, Grand Rapids, MI 49516-6287
www.bakerbooks.com

This book is excerpted from *The Grave Robber*, published in 2014.

Printed in the United States of America

Library of Congress Cataloging-in-Publication Data is on file at the Library of
Congress, Washington, DC.

ISBN 978-0-8010-1663-9

The author is represented by Fedd & Company,
Inc.

In keeping with biblical principles of
creation stewardship, Baker Publishing Group advocates the responsible
use of our natural resources. As a
member of the Green Press Initia-
tive, our company uses recycled
paper when possible. The text paper
of this book is composed in part of
post-consumer waste.

14  15  16  17  18  19  20      7  6  5  4  3  2  1

# Contents

When Mary reached the place where Jesus was and saw him, she fell at his feet and said, "Lord, if you had been here, my brother would not have died."

When Jesus saw her weeping, and the Jews who had come along with her also weeping, he was deeply moved in spirit and troubled. "Where have you laid him?" he asked.

"Come and see, Lord," they replied.

Jesus wept.

Then the Jews said, "See how he loved him!"

But some of them said, "Could not he who opened the eyes of the blind man have kept this man from dying?"

Jesus, once more deeply moved, came to the tomb. It was a cave with a stone laid across the entrance. "Take away the stone," he said.

"But, Lord," said Martha, the sister of the dead man, "by this time there is a bad odor, for he has been there four days."

Then Jesus said, "Did I not tell you that if you believe, you will see the glory of God?"

So they took away the stone. Then Jesus looked up and said, "Father, I thank you that you have heard me. I knew that you always hear me, but I said this for the benefit of the people standing here, that they may believe that you sent me."

When he had said this, Jesus called in a loud voice, "Lazarus, come out!" The dead man came out, his hands and feet wrapped with strips of linen, and a cloth around his face.

Jesus said to them, "Take off the grave clothes and let him go."

John 11:32–44

**1**

# The Grave Robber

*If you had been here, my brother would
not have died. But I know that even now
God will give you whatever you ask.*

John 11:21–22

One of my earliest movie memories is the 1978 version of *Superman* starring Christopher Reeve. Superman's heartthrob, Lois Lane, is driving through the Nevada desert when a crevice opened by an earthquake swallows her car. Superman can't get there in time to save Lois because he's busy building a natural dam out of boulders to stop a flood caused by a breach in the Hoover Dam. When he discovers that Lois is dead, Superman gets super angry. He flies around the earth at supersonic speeds, reversing its rotation, theoretically turning back time.

Now, I know the science behind that scene is suspect. After all, the earth rotates around its axis at one thousand miles per hour. So if Superman had reversed its rotation, he may have saved Lois Lane, but everyone else on the planet would have died of whiplash! But it's still a cool concept, isn't it? Don't you wish you could turn back time right after saying or doing something you wish you hadn't? The problem, of course, is that the arrow of time points in one direction.

What's done is done. Some things in life are irreversible.

You cannot unbake cookies, uncut hair, undelete documents, or unrun red lights. These are a few of the lessons I've learned the hard way. Some of those lessons were easily laughed off after a little embarrassment—like the bald strip on the back of my head after the barber said, "Oops." I actually used Lora's mascara for a few weeks until the bald spot grew back out. Others cost me a little cash, like a $110 ticket for running a red light. Then there are those irreversible moments that leave a hole in your heart forever—like standing at the foot of my father-in-law's casket after a heart attack ended his earthly life at fifty-five years of age.

One of those painful lessons came during my sophomore basketball season in college. Not only did we lose our last game and bow out of the national tournament, but I also tore my anterior cruciate ligament in the second half. When the doctor gave me his diagnosis, I asked him when it would be healed. He said *never*. He told me I needed to have reconstructive surgery because torn ligaments don't heal. At that point in my life basketball *was* my life. So it felt like my life as I knew it was over.

If you've been on the receiving end of divorce papers, received a frantic phone call in the middle of the night, or gotten lab results from your doctor that affirm your worst fears, you know that feeling all too well. And that's precisely how Mary and Martha felt. Their brother was gone for good. And their lives as they knew them were over. But it's not over until God says it's over!

Enter Jesus.

Jesus showed up four days late, but He showed off His power in a way never before witnessed. He had reversed withered arms and weather systems. But this miracle was a sudden-death showdown with an undefeated opponent. The Grave Robber went toe-to-toe with death itself, and death met its match.

## The Law of Entropy

The second law of thermodynamics states that if left to its own devices, everything in the universe moves toward disorder and decay. Cars rust. Food rots. And of course humans grow old and die. It takes many forms, but it's called the law of entropy. And the only way to prevent entropy is to introduce an outside energy source to counteract it. The technical term is negentropy, and the refrigerator is a perfect example. If you plug it into an electrical outlet, it produces cold air that keeps food from rotting. If, however, the refrigerator gets unplugged from its power source, entropy will take over again. This I know from personal experience. Our family returned from a Christmas vacation and I knew something was wrong before we even walked in the front door. We were greeted by a dead refrigerator that smelled like a dead animal. Word to the wise: if your refrigerator dies, keep its door closed.

While we're on the subject of bad odors, that was Mary and Martha's greatest concern when Jesus told the mourners to roll away the stone. They were afraid it would stink to high heaven, but Jesus was about to counteract four days of decomposition with one miracle of negentropy.

The law of entropy doesn't just govern the physical universe. It has governed the spiritual realm since it was introduced in the Garden of Eden after Adam and Eve's original sin. They had been forewarned: "You must not eat from the tree of the knowledge of good and evil, for when you eat from it you will certainly die."[1] While they didn't die immediately after eating the forbidden fruit, their disobedience introduced the process of decay that leads to physical and spiritual death. Sin is a slow-acting poison. Its immediate effects are often indiscernible, but the aftereffects are far more devastating than what we realize at the time. Original sin caused a disturbance in the Force, so to speak. It introduced sickness and suffering to the equation of life. Everything from genetic defects to natural disasters trace their origins back to original sin. We live in a fallen world—everything is affected by entropy.

Just like Adam and Eve discovered, sin opens the door to entropy. The more you sin, the more your life moves toward disorder and decay. Sin is much more than a moral dividing line between right and wrong. It's a matter of life and death. Jesus didn't die on the cross just to make bad people good. He brings dead people to life! And Lazarus is exhibit A.

## Do the Lazarus

To fully appreciate this miracle, you need a basic understanding of ancient Jewish burial traditions. When Lazarus died, his feet would have been bound at the ankles and his arms would have been tied to his body with linen strips. Then his dead body would have been wrapped in approximately one hundred pounds of graveclothes to protect and preserve the body. Some scholars believe that the head itself would have been wrapped with so many linens that it would measure a foot wide. So the best mental image is probably the one that immediately comes to mind—Lazarus looked like a mummy.

Based on Jewish burial traditions, it seems to me like two miracles happen here, not one. The first one is resurrection. But how in the world did Lazarus get up and get out of the tomb in a full-body cast? That's the second miracle! I'm not sure I can re-create the scene, but Lazarus did not walk out of the tomb. I think he hopped out.

> The dead man came out, his hands and feet wrapped with strips of linen, and a cloth around his face.[2]

Maybe my imagination gets a little carried away, but I bet his friends and family "did the Lazarus" at dance parties every chance they got. Lazarus had to bust a move to get out of that tomb. And once again, Jesus turns tragedy into comedy. When Lazarus comes hopping out of the tomb, grieving turns to laughing. And they laughed about it the rest of their lives.

Now let me get serious. If you miss this, you miss the point. This miracle doesn't just foreshadow Jesus' own resurrection. It foreshadows yours! It's not just something Jesus did for Lazarus. It's a snapshot of what Jesus wants to do in your life right here, right now. When we sin, it's like the enemy of our soul wraps us up in graveclothes. Sin buries us alive and makes a mummy out of us. We become a shadow of the person we were meant to be. And if you keep on sinning, it'll weigh you down like a hundred pounds of graveclothes. But Jesus is calling you out of your tomb.

I've found that one of the best ways to personalize the promises in Scripture is to take out the original name and insert your own. And I think it's okay to do that. After all, every promise God has made is *yes* in Christil. So take out Lazarus's name and insert your own: *Mark, come out!*

Can you hear Him call your name?

He's calling you out of sin.

He's calling you out of death.

He's calling you out of your tomb.

## Second Life

Church tradition offers two versions of what happened to Lazarus after his resurrection. One holds that he and his sisters made their way to the island of Cyprus, where Lazarus was the first bishop of Kition. The Church of Saint Lazarus, in the modern city of Larnaca, is believed by some to be built over his second tomb, which he was buried in some thirty years after his first death. A second church tradition holds that Lazarus and his sisters ended up in Marseille,

France, where Lazarus survived the persecution of Christians by Nero by hiding in a tomb, appropriately enough, but eventually died by beheading during the persecution ordered by Emperor Domitian.[4]

I'm not sure which tradition is true or if either of them is. But either way, Jesus gave Mary and Martha their brother back, and Lazarus lived two lives. How long he lived after he died, we don't know for sure. But Jesus gave him a second chance, a second life. And the Grave Robber wants to do for you what He did for Lazarus. But He doesn't just want to give back the life that sin and Satan have stolen. He came that you might have life and have it more abundantly![5] The Son of God entered space-time so that you could exit it—so that you could spend eternity with Him in a place where there is no more mourning or crying or pain. Heaven is the end of entropy as we know it, and death is defeated once and for all. In the words of the apostle Paul:

Where, O death, is your victory?
Where, O death, is your sting?[6]

When my father-in-law died, Parker and Summer were so young that they can't now remember him. So we would often tell stories to help create some memories for our kids. During one of those conversations,

Parker said, "I wish I could have said good-bye to Grandpa and told him to say hi to Jesus." In an overly excited voice, Summer responded, "When we die, we'll get to go to heaven and see Grandpa Schmidgall." To which Parker replied, "You shouldn't get so excited about dying!"

At first that was nothing more than a cute conversation that Lora and I cherished. But over the years I've realized that it's more than that. Remember when Jesus said we must become like little children? I think this is one dimension of that. At some point, the fear of death allays our anticipation of eternal life. But if you've already died to self, you don't have to fear death. You no longer have to live as if the purpose of life is to arrive safely at death.

There is nothing wrong with wanting to live a long life, but death isn't something we dread. Death was defeated two thousand years ago. And to be absent from the body is to be present with the Lord.[7] So death is something we can actually anticipate because it's not the end. It's a new beginning. And many of the miracles we hoped for on earth will finally be fulfilled in heaven.

Our second life begins when Christ calls us out of the tomb of sin. Our eternal life begins when our body is finally buried six feet deep. Death is the exit toll all of us must pay, but it's the entrance ramp to eternity.

## 2

# Even Now

*Lazarus has died, and for your sake I am glad that I was not there.*

John 11:14–15 ESV

I t ranks as one of the most embarrassing moments of my life. It's one thing to forget a wedding you're supposed to attend. It's another thing to forget a wedding you're supposed to officiate! Maybe it's because we didn't do a rehearsal the night before, but it totally slipped my mind.

Have you ever had a phone call trigger your memory? Like an alarm, the ring reminds you of something you were supposed to do or someplace you were supposed to be. The moment my phone rang, my stomach was in my throat because I remembered the noon wedding I was supposed to officiate. It was one o'clock and I was in a dressing room at the mall. I died a thousand deaths in that dressing room! The bride and groom started worrying about their no-show pastor around quarter to noon, but it took more than an hour to track down my cell phone number. And how they got it is nothing short of miraculous. They called the church office, but we're closed on Saturdays. Somehow the call got transferred to the emergency phone in the elevator at our church's coffeehouse, Ebenezer's, and it answered automatically. Our pastor of discipleship, Heather Zempel, happened to be on the elevator when the call came in. She actually thought it was a crank call because she couldn't imagine me forgetting a wedding, but I was guilty as charged.

I showered like Speedy Gonzales, threw on a suit like Superman, and drove to the wedding venue like it was the NASCAR Sprint Cup Series. I arrived at 3:00 sharp, and the ceremony commenced. It wasn't easy making eye contact with the wedding guests, but the bride and groom were unbelievably gracious. In fact, they still attend our church. Don't tell me miracles don't happen!

When I finally got there, I decided not to say what Jesus said when He was late to Lazarus's funeral. I did *not* say, "For your sake, I am glad I was not there."[1]

Why on earth would Jesus say that?

It seems thoughtless at best and heartless at worst. If your friend is on his deathbed and you have the ability to heal him, don't you drop everything and get there as quickly as possible? Yet Jesus stays put for two days. Then He takes His sweet time getting there. And the question is, *why*?

## Passive-Aggressive

When Jesus finally shows up four days late, Mary and Martha get a little passive-aggressive with him. They both say the same exact thing: "If you had been here, my brother would not have died."[2] They aren't really blaming Jesus . . . but they are, but they aren't, but they are. And the truth is, we all have passive-aggressive tendencies toward God, don't we? We don't blame Him for the bad things that happen, but we also know He could have kept them from happening. So why doesn't He?

Why wouldn't Jesus just teleport to Bethany and heal Lazarus?

My take is this: Jesus had been there and done that. Jesus could have walked across water, arrived in the nick of time, and healed Lazarus as he was drawing his last breath. But Jesus had already revealed His healing power. It was time to unveil His *resurrection power*.

You cannot resurrect what has not died. So Jesus waited a little longer to reveal a little more of His power. And He does the same thing with us. If you feel like you're in a holding pattern, it may be because God is getting ready to do something more miraculous than you've previously experienced. But something precious might have to die first so that He can resurrect it.

If Jesus had simply healed Lazarus, I'm sure some people would have praised God. I'm also sure some skeptics would have claimed he wasn't really that sick to begin with or credited his recovery to the miracle of medicine. But when someone has been dead for four days, there is only one logical and theological explanation. You have witnessed a miracle of the first order.

If Jesus had simply healed Lazarus, it would have reinforced the faith they already had. Jesus wanted to stretch their faith. And in order to do that, sometimes things have to go from bad to worse before they get better!

## God's Grammar

I've forgotten most of the sermons I've heard, and I'm sure our congregation has forgotten most of mine. But every once in a while, there is a moment of revelation in the middle of a message that is life altering. That's what I experienced listening to an old sermon by Dr. Charles Crabtree titled "God's Grammar." I found one little line to be absolutely unforgettable: "Never put a comma where God puts a period and never put a period where God puts a comma."

When someone dies, we naturally put a period on it. Game over. But Jesus knew He would take it into overtime with a Hail Mary, so to speak. When He heard the news that Lazarus was sick, Jesus made a bold prediction: "This sickness will not end in death."[3] I used to have a problem with that statement because it seems like Jesus is wrong, right? After all, Lazarus does in fact die. But the operative word is *end*. Jesus said the sickness would not end in death, and it didn't. He knew Lazarus would die, but Jesus didn't put a period there. He inserted a four-day comma.

"Sometimes it looks like God is missing the mark," observed Oswald Chambers, "because we're too short-sighted to see what He's aiming for."[4]

Have you ever felt like God was a day late and a dollar short?

Mary and Martha felt like He was four days late! The window of opportunity closed when Lazarus drew his last breath, but it's not over until God says it's over! God always gets the final word. And Martha knew it. What comes out of her mouth ranks as one of the greatest statements of faith in all of Scripture:

> Lord . . . if you had been here, my brother would not have died. But I know that even now God will give you whatever you ask.[5]

Did you catch the conjunction? There is a *but* between her statement of fact and her statement of faith.

Evidently, Martha is still holding out hope four days after the funeral. To be honest, a psychotherapist might diagnose this as a psychotic break. After all, denial ain't just a river in Egypt. At what point do you stop hoping and start grieving? Day one? Day two? Day four? Some would say it was her grief speaking, but she was speaking out of *faith*. Faith often looks like it's out of touch with reality, but that's because it's in touch with a reality that is more real than anything you can see or hear or taste or touch or smell with your five senses. Faith is our sixth sense. And if you're truly in touch with God, sometimes it'll appear as if you are out of touch with reality.

The sentence should end after Martha says, "Lord, if you had been here my brother would not have died." But Martha doesn't put a period there. Faith inserts a comma, even at the end of a death sentence. That's what Martha does: "Even now God will give you whatever you ask."

I love the little phrase embedded in this statement of faith: *even now*. It's one of my favorite phrases in all of Scripture. Even when it seems like God is four days late, it's too soon to give up. Even when it seems like your dream is dead and buried, don't put a period there.

## Here Comes the Boom

Susanna Wright and her husband minister in one of the poorest areas of London. During a difficult season of ministry, Susanna lost the very hope she offered. And it was compounded by the fact that her dream of having her book published was all but dead. In her words, "I forgot about the resurrection." And the same thing happens to us, doesn't it? Many Christians remember the resurrection once a year! The rest of the year we live as if Jesus is still nailed to the cross.

When Susanna hit bottom, she picked up a copy of *The Circle Maker*, and God resurrected her writing dream. Like so many aspiring authors, Susanna didn't know a single soul in the publishing industry. So breaking into that industry felt like breaking into Buckingham Palace.

One day Susanna was scouring the website of an international publishing house when she discovered that their UK office was in London, just two miles from her home. She decided to circle their office building every week, praying for a way in. Week in and week out, Susanna prayed morning, noon, and night. Then one morning she threw down the gauntlet with God. She said, "Lord, I'm sick of praying day and night for a breakthrough. I want to feel the boom that Mark Batterson talks about."

Susanna was referencing the part in *The Circle Maker* where I shared the science behind a sonic boom and likened it to the breakthrough we experience when we pray through. Almost like a sonic boom, there comes a moment in prayer when you know that God has answered your prayer. While the answer may not be a physical reality yet, you know it's just a matter of time before God delivers on His promise.

Just as Susanna prayed for that boom, a London double-decker drove up, painted with a bus-size billboard that simply said, "Here comes the boom!" Susanna started laughing out loud as people stood and stared at her. Once she regained her composure, Susanna took a picture of the bus and hung it in her kitchen. Shortly thereafter, the publisher Susanna had been circling in prayer offered to publish her book. She says:

> All my life, I have written. I wrote my first poem at seven; sent off my first story to a children's publisher when I was eleven; and now, I will be a published writer. I have experienced a revival I did not think possible in my heart. God has somehow set my life right again. He has opened the doors of a major publishing house and launched a writing ministry that has been brewing in me for nearly three decades.

When it comes to God-ordained dreams, I can almost guarantee that they will take longer and be harder to accomplish than you ever imagined. By definition, a God-ordained dream will always be beyond your ability and beyond your resources. But that is how God gets the glory. If you feel like your dream is dead and buried, maybe God has you right where He wants you. Almost every dream I've ever had has gone through a death and resurrection. It's the litmus test. If it's not from God, it'll stay dead. If it is, it'll rise again. But you need to pray through until you experience the breakthrough.

Here comes the boom!

## Not Yet

When God says no to a prayer, it doesn't always mean no. Sometimes it means *not yet*. It's the right request but the wrong time.

A few years ago Lora and I were house hunting on Capitol Hill. We had lived on the Hill since 1996 when we were fortunate enough to buy a hundred-year-old home during a buyer's market. As our kids got bigger, our fifteen-foot-wide row home got smaller, so we started looking for a little more elbow room. We found our dream home less than a block away.

Lora and I decided to make an offer, but we also knew our financial limits. After praying about it, we came up with our best offer and felt like it was a fleece. If God wanted us to have the house, the owner would accept our offer. With the real estate market lagging and the time on the market mounting, we were confident the seller would accept our offer. He did not. And as much as we wanted the house, and as tempted as we were to go beyond our predetermined offer, we made the difficult decision to walk away. And we stopped looking at homes.

One night about a year later, as we drove by the home we had tried to purchase, Lora said, "Do you ever feel like that is the one that got away?" We had driven by it a hundred times since the owner rejected our offer, and we had never said so much as a word about it. It was dead to us. But Lora's casual comment must have been a prophetic prayer, because the very next morning there was a For Sale sign in the yard. That's when I had a holy hunch that God's *no* a year earlier was really a *not yet*.

What Lora and I didn't know was that the owner had never sold the house. It sat on the market for 252 days with no buyer, so it was taken off the market. When the same owner put the house back on the market, we decided to make the same offer. It was a calculated risk because he'd already said no once, but it was another fleece. We told our real estate agent it was our first and final offer. We were willing to walk away a second time, but we didn't have to. God answered our prayer a full year after we thought He would.

Most miracles take longer than we want, but the longer we wait, the more we appreciate them. I hope your miracle doesn't take thirty-eight years like the one for the invalid in John 5, but no matter how long it takes, you need to trust God's timing. Miracles happen once we're good and ready, and not a moment sooner. Sometimes it's because God in His grace is allowing us to mature so we'll be able to steward it. Sometimes He waits so we don't miss the point. And sometimes God waits to punctuate His power.

Having gone through a death and resurrection with our dream home has made us appreciate it more than we would have otherwise. It also ensures that we own our house, not the other way around. When something is given back after it is taken away, whether it's a house or our health, we don't take it for granted. It's like having your cake and eating it too! In our case, God even put some icing on it. Because we waited a year to buy our new home, our old home actually went up in value by 10 percent because the real estate market in DC rebounded. So we got our new home for the same amount of money and sold our old house for a lot more money than we would have a year earlier! Tithing on the sale of our house was one of the easiest checks we've ever written because God's hand of favor was so evident.

## Second-Degree Faith

Let me double back to Martha's statement of faith:

> Lord . . . if you had been here, my brother would not have died. But I know that even now God will give you whatever you ask.[6]

This one statement reveals two types of faith.

The first half is what I call *preventative faith*. Martha says, "Lord, if you had been here, my brother would not have died."[7] Preventative faith believes God can keep things from happening. So we pray for traveling mercies or a hedge of protection around our children. And while there is nothing wrong with that, there is a second dimension of faith that believes that God can actually undo what's been done. I call it *resurrection faith*. It's a faith that refuses to put periods at the end of disappointments because God can make your impossible possible. Even when the application is denied or the adoption falls through or the business goes bankrupt, you don't put a period there. Even then you believe *even now*.

At some point, most of us end up with a dream that is buried six feet under failure. In fact, that's true of nearly every dream God has ever given me!

When I was in college, I dreamed of planting a church and pastoring it for life. I've been living that dream for seventeen years as the lead pastor of National Community Church in Washington, DC, but there is a prequel. My first attempt was a complete failure. When I was in seminary, the dream of planting a church in Chicago turned into a nightmare. The good news is that when that dream died, part of my ego died with it. Few things kill pride faster than failure! And that's the point. God doesn't want to kill the dream He's given you, but He does want to crucify anything that would keep Him from getting all of the glory when you ultimately succeed.

There are times when you need to hang on to a dream for dear life, but there are also times when a dream needs to be laid to rest. And it takes discernment to know the difference. I suppose Mary and Martha could have kept Lazarus lying in state on his deathbed instead of embalming him and laying him in the tomb. But their human attempt to make a miracle easier would have actually robbed God of the opportunity to reveal His resurrection power! It's one thing raising the dead off of their deathbed. It's another thing calling a dead man out of a tomb four days postmortem!

What needs to die so that it can be resurrected? So that God can reveal more of His power? So that God gets all of the glory?

You need to bury it.
Then if it's resurrected, you know God did it.

It takes courage to end an unhealthy dating relationship, but you won't find Mr. Right as long as you are dating Mr. Wrong. It takes courage to quit a job, but it might be the difference between making a living and making a life. It takes courage to change majors, but it's better to fail at something you love than to succeed at something you hate. Maybe you need to bury the relationship, bury the job, or bury the major. Then you need to wait for Jesus to show up.

Over the past year and a half, I've prayed for someone in our church who felt called to quit his job during a forty-day prayer challenge. After filling out more than 330 job applications with no offers, he second-guessed his decision more than a time or two. Faith turned to doubt, then doubt turned to depression. "Turns out my forty-day prayer challenge went into overtime!" he told me. More like double overtime! Then, just when he felt as if he was unemployable, he beat out fifty other applicants for his dream job. "I don't know why I had a seventeen-month time-out," he confessed. "But since I'm single, my career was by far the most important thing in my life. Maybe that's why God took it away temporarily."

When God takes something away from us, it doesn't always mean that He takes it away forever. In fact, God often takes things away with the express purpose of giving them back. And when He does, we're able to see the miracle for what it is. If you've lost love and found it again, you know whereof I speak. The same is true of health and wealth. It's much more difficult to take the blessing for granted.

## Jesus Wept

It was customary in ancient Israel to bury someone on the day of death. After death, the Talmud prescribed seven days of deep mourning and thirty days of light mourning. So Jesus shows up right in the middle of their deepest sorrow and grieves with them. John 11:35 simply says:

Jesus wept.

It's one of the shortest verses in the Bible, but it speaks volumes. And I'm not sure the English translation does it justice. The force of the Greek verb tense suggests that Jesus burst into tears. This was no measured response. Jesus literally lost it. It reveals how much Jesus loved Lazarus. It also reveals a God who sheds tears! And He doesn't just cry over us, He collects our tears in a bottle.[8]

Your tears are precious to God. Whether they are tears of joy, tears of sorrow, or tears of pain—not one teardrop is lost on God.

If you've endured the type of loss Mary and Martha experienced, you know that sometimes you just need a shoulder to cry on. I'm grateful for those friends who seem to show up when everybody else disappears. Jesus is a friend who sticks closer than a brother,[9] and His broad shoulders can bear any burden. But sometimes you need more than a listening ear, more than a shoulder to cry on. You need a friend *who can do something about your situation.* The good news is: Jesus is both.

Jesus doesn't just get sad. The Son of God gets mad. Death was never part of God's original plan. It was the fallout from the fall. Jesus is good and angry because death has stolen His friend. So the Grave Robber steals him back!

# 3

# Risk Your Reputation

*Jesus, once more deeply moved, came to the tomb. It was a cave with a stone laid across the entrance. "Take away the stone," he said.*

*"But, Lord," said Martha, the sister of the dead man, "by this time there is a bad odor, for he has been there four days."*

John 11:38–39

When he was twenty-five years old, evangelist Clayton King led a fifty-mile backpacking trip into the Himalaya mountains to share the gospel with an unreached people group in the Zanskar Valley.[1] Along with the physical challenge of making the mountainous hike, the risk of being kidnapped or killed was very real. Just a few months before their trip, a group of European missionaries were executed by Islamic militants for attempting to smuggle eleven Bibles across the border. Clayton and his friends had *eleven hundred* Bibles in their backpacks!

In preparation for their missionary journey, the team did water-only fasts, trained with weighted backpacks, and read as much as they could about Tibetan Buddhism. One of the team members was a doctor, so they manufactured a mobile medical clinic to take with them. And last but not least, they prayed for miracles, because they knew they'd need them. Lots of them.

The five-person team flew into Leh, one of the highest airports in the world. After acclimating to the 11,000-foot elevation, they traveled along the Kashmiri border with Pakistan toward the remote village of Zangla. On the way there, one divine appointment set the tone for the rest of the trip. In the middle of nowhere, they came across a hitchhiker who was standing by the side of the road. For all they knew, this man could be a terrorist, so the team protested when their native-born driver pulled over to pick him up. Clayton objected so vehemently that the hitchhiker said in his broken English, "You are a very loud-talking boy." Then he revealed why the driver stopped: "My name is Raja Norbu, and I am the king of the Zanskar Valley. I live in a small village called Zangla. It is very far from here and difficult to reach. As provincial governor, I must attend annual meetings in the capital of Delhi. I was on my way there when my vehicle broke down. Your driver recognized me as King Norbu."

What are the odds?

I don't know about you, but I've met exactly zero kings! And Clayton didn't just meet a king, he met the king of the very village his team was trying to reach!

Sometimes God shows up. Sometimes God shows off.

After revealing who he was, the king of Zangla asked Clayton's name. When he replied, "Clayton King," King Norbu took him literally! When he asked why an American king would visit his village, Clayton didn't pull any punches. He told the king that they wanted to set up a medical clinic and give his people copies of their holy book, the Bible. King Norbu was so pleased that he gave Clayton a handwritten letter that not only ensured safe passage and a warm reception in Zangla but also named Clayton the interim king while he was away. So when the team arrived in Zangla, they were treated like, you guessed it, kings!

## A Show of Power

The second day in the village, the queen asked Clayton if he knew how to deliver a baby. Clayton had no clue, but the medical doctor on their team certainly did. She examined the mother and her twin babies, quickly assessing the situation. It was a high-risk pregnancy to begin with, but to complicate matters, the first baby was breech. And in the doctor's professional opinion, the baby had already died in utero.

Clayton isn't sure what came over him in that moment, but he asked his interpreter to translate a message. It wasn't until after the words were already out of his mouth that he realized the potential ramifications. With the boldness of an Old Testament prophet, Clayton said:

> We have come from America as the people of God. Our God is Jesus Christ, who was killed for our sins and then raised from the dead. He's powerful and loving, and He will show you His power. This mother will live tonight. And these babies will live tonight. God has sent us to you for this purpose. If they die, then you can do with us anything you wish.

In order to deliver the baby who was in a breech position, the doctor had to break his hip. While that enabled the baby to be born, he was in fact stillborn. There was no pulse, no heartbeat, and no breath. They didn't know how long the baby had been dead, but Clayton did the only thing he knew how to do. He cried out to God like his life depended on it, and there was a good chance that his life did depend on it. The next few minutes proved to be the most poignant moments of Clayton's life. After what felt like four days, the Grave Robber did it again. God raised the dead right in front of their eyes. This stillborn baby let out a scream that was music to their ears!

In cultures that are superstitious or animistic, God will often reveal Himself with what missiologists call "a show of power." The showdown between Elijah and the prophets of Baal in 1 Kings 18 is a great example. It was like a prophetic cage fight with no holds barred. There was even some smack talk! And just as God proved His superior power to Baal worshipers, He proved His power to a village of Tibetan Buddhists by raising a baby from the dead.

## Come Out

If you've read the Bible from cover to cover, you suffer from hindsight bias. You know how every story ends, so it's hard to imagine an alternate outcome. Not only do you lose the element of surprise, but you also lose the raw emotion. And that's certainly true of this miracle.

If you can, try to forget how this story ends. Now put yourself within earshot of Jesus when He says, "Lazarus, come out!"[2] You hear the words come out of His mouth, but you can hardly believe your ears!

Who talks to dead people as if they can hear you?

Who has the audacity to demand that the grave give up its dead?

Because we assume the outcome—Lazarus walking out of the tomb—we fail to appreciate the risk Jesus took. If Lazarus remains dead, this ranks as Jesus' most embarrassing moment. And the family and friends who had gathered to grieve are the victims of a cruel joke!

Don't miss this little subplot in this story line.

The six miracles that precede this one in John's Gospel certainly establish Jesus' credibility. He reveals His mastery over everything from water molecules to the four dimensions of space-time reality. But just like the world of athletics or entertainment, you're only as good as your last game or last performance. If Lazarus doesn't walk out of the tomb, Jesus' credibility is out the window. So when Jesus called Lazarus out, He was pushing all of His miraculous chips to the middle of the table and betting it all on Lazarus. The stakes could not have been any higher, but that's how most miracles happen.

## The Hand of God

Do you know why most of us don't experience miracles? It's because we never put ourselves in situations that necessitate one! We comfort the grieving instead of calling dead people out of the tomb. But if we took a few more risks, we might see a few more miracles! And that's one more secret to experiencing the miraculous: *you have to risk your reputation.*

Sometimes you need to lay your credibility on the line! That's what Jesus did when He called Lazarus out of the tomb. That's what Clayton did when he proclaimed that those twin babies would live. And isn't that what Shadrach, Meshach, and Abednego did when they refused to bow down to a ninety-foot idol?[3]

They knew they'd be executed if they didn't bow down, but they feared God more than they feared death itself. They would rather die by the flame than dishonor God. So they defied the earthly king with a bold declaration:

> King Nebuchadnezzar, we do not need to defend ourselves before you in this matter. If we are thrown into the blazing furnace, the God we serve is able to deliver us from it, and he will deliver us from Your Majesty's hand. But even if he does not, we want you to know, Your Majesty, that we will not serve your gods.[4]

To be honest, I could have come up with a dozen rationalizations to justify bowing down. "I'm bowing on the outside, but I'm not bowing on the inside." "I'll ask for forgiveness right after I get back up." "My fingers are crossed." "I'm only breaking one of the Ten Commandments." "What good am I to God if I'm dead?" When it comes to sinful rationalizations, we are infinitely creative, aren't we? But it's our rationalizations that often annul His miraculous intervention. When we compromise our integrity, we don't leave room for divine intervention. When we take matters into our own hands, we take God out of the equation. When we try to manipulate a situation, we miss out on the miracle.

Stop and think about it.

If Shadrach, Meshach, and Abednego had bowed down to the statue, they would have been delivered from the fiery furnace. But it would have been by the hand of man, not the hand of God. And while they would have saved their lives, they would have sacrificed their integrity. They also would have forfeited the miracle.

When we bow down to what's wrong, we put our reputation and God's reputation at risk. But when we stand up for what's right, we establish God's reputation by putting ourselves in a posture where God can show up and show off. And God does just that.

> Not a hair on their heads was singed, and their clothing was not scorched. They didn't even smell of smoke![5]

## A Double Miracle

I did a radio interview shortly after *The Circle Maker* was released, and the host told me an amazing story about his missionary friend, Dr. Bob Bagley. Bob's church in Africa didn't have a church building, so they gathered under the shade of a single tree near the village. That is, until the local witch doctor cursed the tree. When it withered and died, the church didn't just lose their shade. They were overshadowed by the curse because it undermined the authority of their message.

Bob knew their status in the village was in jeopardy if he didn't do something about it, so he called for a public prayer meeting. Not unlike Elijah, who challenged the prophets of Baal to a prayer duel, Bob confronted the curse and called down a blessing on the tree that had died. He literally laid hands on the tree trunk and prayed that God would resurrect it.

It was a calculated risk, but every prayer is, isn't it? If God didn't answer Bob's prayer, he would have dug an even deeper hole! But if you don't ask for the miracle, you'll never know what God might have done. Again, God won't answer 100 percent of the prayers you don't pray. If you don't get the answer you prayed for, it's not a fail. After all, the answer is up to God. Prayer is the way we put the ball in God's court. The only way you can fail is by failing to ask.

Now having said that, let me say this: if you're going to call someone out of a tomb, you'd better make sure you heard from God. The same is true if you're going to lay hands on a tree or prophesy that a stillborn baby will live. But if God speaks, you'd better not remain silent.

Bob asked God to resurrect the tree, but I love the little tagline he added at the end of his prayer: "It's not my name that's at stake."

When you act in faith, it may seem like you are risking your reputation, but it's really God's reputation that's at stake. And God is able to defend His name, His reputation. As I survey Scripture, it seems to me that those God uses the most are those who risk their reputation the most. They aren't afraid to ask God to make the sun stand still, walls fall down, or an iron ax head float.

The way you establish God's reputation is by risking your own. If you don't take the risk, you'll never witness the kind of miracles Bob did. God didn't just break the curse and resurrect the tree. It became the only tree of its type to yield its fruit not once but twice a year.

A double crop.
A double blessing.
A double miracle.

## The Ultimate Apologetic

This miracle reveals the true identity, the full identity of Jesus. He's more than the Wine Maker or the

Water Walker. He's the Grave Robber. And He saves
His boldest claim for last:

I am the resurrection and the life.[6]

It's that unique claim that sets Jesus apart and puts
Him in a category by Himself: the Son of God. Christianity is not built on the foundation of philosophy or
a code of ethics. The footer of our faith is one funda-
mental fact—the empty tomb. After cheating death
by calling Lazarus out of his tomb, Jesus walked out
of His own tomb under His own power! That's the
ultimate apologetic—there is no argument against it.

If the resurrection didn't happen, Christianity ranks
as history's cruelest hoax. We're not just wasting our
lives worshiping Him. We're living a lie. But if Jesus
walked out of the tomb two thousand years ago, all
bets are off. Or maybe I should say, all bets are on Jesus.

There is an old saying: *no one ever bet too much on a
winning horse.* The winning horse is the White Horse
that Jesus will ride when He returns for His church.[7]

Thomas Jefferson had a profound appreciation for
the teachings of Jesus, but Jefferson was also a child of
the Enlightenment, and as such he enthroned reason
and made logic lord. In February 1804, Jefferson went
to work with a razor. He clipped his favorite passages
out of his Bible and pasted them in double columns on

forty-six octavo sheets. Jefferson included the teachings of Jesus but excluded the miracles. He deleted the virgin birth, the resurrection, and every supernatural event in between. Jefferson's version of the Gospels comes to a dead end when the stone is rolled in front of the tomb on Good Friday. And I think that is where most people leave Jesus. Most people have no hesitation acknowledging that Jesus was compassionate and wise, a great teacher or a powerful prophet. But that isn't who He claimed to be. He claimed to be the resurrection and the life. And that's where many people get stuck. But we're only left with two options: either Jesus was who He claimed to be or He wasn't. There is no middle ground.

In an interview with *Rolling Stone* magazine, Bono was asked his opinion on Jesus with this question: "Christ has His rank among the world's greatest thinkers. But Son of God, isn't that far-fetched?" The lead singer of U2 and global crusader against poverty responded:

No, it's not far-fetched to me. Look, the secular response to the Christ story always goes like this. He was a great prophet who had a lot to say along the lines of other great prophets, be they Elijah, Muhammad, Buddha, or Confucius. But actually Christ doesn't allow you that. He doesn't let you off that hook. Christ says, "No. I'm not saying I'm a teacher, don't call me a teacher. I'm not saying I'm a prophet. I'm saying: I'm the Messiah. I'm saying: I am God incarnate." And people say: No, no, please, just be a prophet. A prophet we can take. So what you're left with is either Christ was who He said he was—the Messiah—or a complete nutcase.[8]

Imagine a Jefferson vs. Bono debate. I'd pay-per-view to see that. I'm guessing the oddsmakers would make Jefferson the favorite by a long shot, but I think Bono wins this debate. While most people, like Jefferson, have no issue accepting Jesus as a compassionate healer or wise teacher or even a religious prophet, that isn't who He alleged to be. He claimed to be the Son of God. And as C. S. Lewis famously observed, Jesus is either a liar, a lunatic, or in fact who He claimed to be—Lord.[9]

There is no middle ground. Either Jesus is Lord of all or He's not Lord at all. So which is it? That one decision will determine your eternal destiny. It will also make the impossible possible!

## 4

# One Little Yes

*Do you believe this?*

John 11:26

After asserting His identity as the resurrection and the life, Jesus pops a point-blank question that punctuates Martha's life: "Do you believe this?"[1] Remember: Jesus hadn't called Lazarus out of the tomb quite yet, so Martha was still in the depths of despair. Hope was four days dead. Yet Martha responds with her simple profession of faith:

Yes, Lord.[2]

One little *yes* can change your life.
One little *yes* can change your eternity.

The litmus test is the same now as it was then. The only question on God's final exam is: *Do you believe this?* It's not a multiple-choice question. It's true or false. And it's the most important question you'll ever answer. That one decision will determine your eternal destiny. The good news is that it's an open-book exam, and God reveals the right answer in Romans 10:9:

> If you confess with your mouth that Jesus is Lord and believe in your heart that God raised him from the dead, you will be saved. (ESV)

The resurrection of Jesus Christ is the axis around which our faith revolves. When Jesus rose from the dead, it radically redefined reality. When He walked out of the tomb under His own power, the word *impossible* was removed from our vocabulary. The resurrection is the history-changer, the game-changer. But the trick is learning to live as if Jesus was crucified yesterday, rose from the dead today, and is coming back tomorrow![3]

The resurrection isn't something we celebrate once a year by donning an Easter bonnet. It's something we celebrate every day in every way. The resurrection of dead bodies is nothing short of miraculous, and the rematerialization of dead bodies when Christ returns is going to be must-see TV. But the resurrection miracles don't stop there. God raises dreams from the dead. He resurrects dead relationships. And no matter what part of your personality has died at the hands of sin or suffering or Satan himself, the Grave Robber came to give you your life back!

No one had laughed or smiled since the day Lazarus was laid to rest. When he walked out of the tomb, no one could stop. This miracle is a snapshot of who Jesus is, what Jesus does. The Grave Robber steals back what the enemy has stolen. Then He gives it back to us, with interest.

A few years ago I had the privilege of baptizing a young woman whose life had been totally transformed by the grace of God. I'll never forget Rachel's face when she came back up out of the water. Pure joy! Rachel described it this way: "Now I'm the person I was as a child, always smiling and laughing."

When Jesus died on the cross, Satan smiled. But the Grave Robber got the last laugh. He always does. And if you give Him a chance, He'll give you a second chance.

He will give you your smile back.
He will give you your laugh back.
He will give you your life back.

*Do you believe this?*

If you do, He will make the impossible possible.

# Notes

### Chapter 1  The Grave Robber

1. Genesis 2:17.
2. John 11:44.
3. See 2 Corinthians 1:20.
4. "What Happened to Lazarus after His Resurrection?" *The Straight Dope*, October 20, 2009, http://www.straightdope.com/columns/read/2902/what-happened-to-lazarus-after-his-resurrection.
5. See John 10:10 ESV.
6. 1 Corinthians 15:55.
7. See 2 Corinthians 5:8.

### Chapter 2  Even Now

1. John 11:15.
2. John 11:21, 32.
3. John 11:4.

4. Oswald Chambers, "The Big Compelling of God," in *My Utmost for His Highest*, http://utmost.org/classic/the-big-compelling-of-god-classic/.

5. John 11:21–22.

6. Ibid.

7. See John 11:21.

8. See Psalm 56:8 ESV.

9. See Proverbs 18:24.

## Chapter 3 Risk Your Reputation

1. Clayton told me this story in person, but you can read his amazing account in his book *Amazing Encounters with God: Stories to Open Your Eyes to His Power* (Eugene, OR: Harvest House, 2009).

2. John 11:43.

3. See Daniel 3.

4. Daniel 3:16–18.

5. Daniel 3:27 NLT.

6. John 11:25.

7. See Revelation 19:11.

8. Michka Assayas, *Bono: In Conversation with Michka Assayas* (New York: Riverhead, 2005), 205.

9. C. S. Lewis, *Mere Christianity* (1952; New York: HarperCollins, 2001), 54.

## Chapter 4 One Little Yes

1. See John 11:25–26.

2. John 11:27 NLT.

3. Thanks to Martin Luther for this thought. He said, "Preach as if Jesus was crucified yesterday, rose from the dead today, and is coming back tomorrow."

**Mark Batterson** is the *New York Times* bestselling author of *The Circle Maker*. The lead pastor of National Community Church in Washington, DC, Mark has a doctor of ministry degree from Regent University and lives on Capitol Hill with his wife, Lora, and their three children.

■ ■ ■
Connect with
MARK
BATTERSON
at
MarkBatterson.com

@MarkBatterson

Mark Batterson

@MarkBatterson

Connect with National Community Church at
**WWW.THEATERCHURCH.COM**

"Mark reminds us that faith in
Jesus is worth the risk."

—MAX LUCADO, pastor and bestselling author

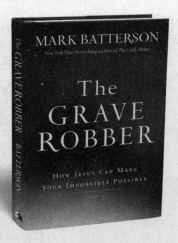

Sometimes it's hard to believe that God still
does miracles. We don't expect Him to move
in miraculous ways in our day-in and day-out
lives. Maybe we'd like to see miracles,
but it's hard to see past our problems.

All that is about to change,
like water into wine.

# Perfect for Your Small Group

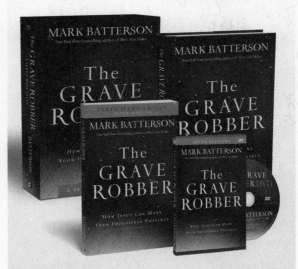

Perfect for a church-wide experience or a small group. *The Grave Robber* will help congregations discover that **God can still do the impossible**.

# Your students can experience God's power today.

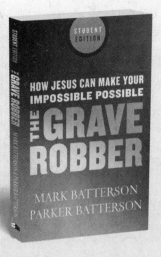

Mark Batterson has teamed up with his teenage son, Parker, to tell true stories of the miraculous.